Table of Contents

Problem

- Decreased defense spending necessitates leveraging and globalizing resources.
- The United States Air Force lacks the ability to leverage resources through virtual team operations, collaborative interfaces, and global data management.

Methodology

- Interviews with 20 members of the Air Force Smart Operations for the 21st Century virtual team.

Major Findings

- Virtual teams require a clearly defined purpose and agreed upon charter.
- Virtual teams must identify a team leader.
- Teams need to select collaborative tools that fit their overall team purpose.
- Team members need training on virtual communication, conflict resolution and collaboration tools.

Recommendations

- **Team Sponsor** – Team sponsors must define a clear purpose for why the virtual team has been created, establish the team leader, and build support for the team's operations across the organization.
- **Leaders** – Virtual team leaders need to ensure the team has an agreed upon team charter that defines the expectations of team members. Additionally, team leaders must take proactive steps to ensure the collaborative tools used by the team function properly and as needed. Finally, virtual team leaders need to apply the correct leadership style to maximize team performance and seek opportunities to further collaboration across the team's membership.
- **Team Members** – Virtual team members must clarify expectations regarding team and individual performance. Furthermore, team members need to take an active role in testing, evaluating, and selecting the most appropriate collaborative tools that fit the team's process. Finally, the team membership should seek to incorporate subject matter experts as activities warrant their inclusion.

What does this really mean?

- **Why should leaders care?** Leaders establish the tone of team operations affecting collaboration and ultimately how well a virtual team can leverage and globalize resources.
- **How should leaders and team members change?** Virtual team participants need to understand that working on a virtual team is different from traditional face-to-face teams in terms of communication and collaboration. However, both teams still require strong leadership and a clear team charter.

What results can be expected if leaders and team members change?
The sharing of knowledge and expertise across global boundaries can offset resource constraints, develop solutions to problems faster, and improve overall organizational performance allowing the Air Force to globalize operations in previously unimagined ways.

Virtual Team Leadership in the United States Air Force

On 29 September 2008, Dr. Ritter provided authorization for a study on the Air Force Smart Operations for the 21st Century (AFSO21) virtual team. The virtual team was created to provide a means for Air Staff Agencies and major commands to cross-flow information related to AFSO21 transformation initiatives, thereby leveraging knowledge and expertise across the Air Force. The purpose of the study was to gain an understanding of how the virtual team operated and develop a strategic plan related to the operation of future virtual teams.

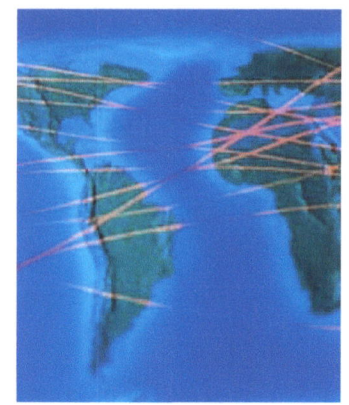

The study relied on interviews with 20 AFSO21 virtual team members randomly selected from the team roster. Interviews provided insight into the team's operation and resulted in the development of several recommendations related to virtual team operations, leadership, and collaboration. Implementing these recommendations will enhance future virtual team efforts in the United States Air Force (USAF) and other agencies in the Department of Defense (DOD).

Problem and Purpose

The United States military environment is not prepared to defend and respond to non-traditional threats to national security, such as nuclear terrorism and information network attacks (Rubin, 2007; White House, 2009). The number of personnel in the USAF has decreased by 44.3% since 1986 (Faykes, 2007), and the scrutiny of increased defense spending necessitates the leveraging and globalization of resources; these concerns represent a departure from conventional Cold War-era defense strategies (AFP Press, 2009; Frost, 2008; Miles, 2009).

In particular, the USAF is not prepared to defend and respond to threats to national security using virtual teams as a means to create collaborative interfaces with global divisions, employ budgetary efficiencies, or create data management, information, and communication strategies (Seymour & Cowen, 2006). The USAF lacks an online environment with an integrated approach to facilitate virtual collaboration (Seymour & Cowen, 2006) from which to explore, discover and predict common United States Air Force defense strategies and realities (Haselkorn, 2007).

The purpose of this study was to explore the perceptions, understandings, and lived experiences of the Air Force Smart Operations for the 21st Century virtual team members. Additionally, this study sought to explore an integrated approach to facilitate virtual collaboration that will globalize resources. Finally, developing an implementation plan for the future application of virtual teams was a desired outcome for this study.

Significance of Study

The four main elements contributing to the significance of this research study were responding to global change, virtual team operation, the process of military transformation, and the application of virtual teams in the USAF. The need to transform the military is in response to a rapidly changing global environment (Garmone, 2001). The prevalence of non-traditional threats to national security necessitates the Department of Defense (DOD) leverage its resources more effectively. Virtual teams are one approach organizations can take to leverage resources. Virtual teams require a non-traditional approach to leadership for them to succeed while transformation requires a change of mindset, culture, and attitude (Office of Assistant Secretary for Public Affairs, 2005). Exploring the use of virtual teams helped identify one aspect of the USAF's ability to meet current and future national security requirements.

Understanding the implications of how virtual teams operate in the USAF can contribute to the transformation efforts of the other services as they seek to leverage resources in a rapidly changing world. The leadership of virtual teams requires leaders serve as facilitators, moving them from traditional positional-based leadership roles to becoming information clearinghouses for their team (Larue & Childs, 2006). Uncovering if the USAF was able to shift its leadership approach to embrace leaders as facilitators versus traditional positional based leaders may influence the field of leadership.

Virtual teams present several benefits over traditional teams. One benefit includes cost savings since employees working on virtual teams do not need to travel to attend meetings (Carew & Parisi-Carew, 2006). Another benefit is they permit global collaboration on projects (Carew & Parisi-Carew, 2006). Global collaboration allows organizations to employ the most skilled employees across their organization to solve problems instead of being limited to personnel at a specific geographic location. Furthermore, organizations can leverage intellectual capital by pulling employees together across the globe onto a single virtual team. A third benefit of virtual teams is they can increase productivity. They accomplish this in two ways, first, virtual teams are able to operate 24 hours a day since some of the global team members are at work at any

given time (Carew & Parisi-Carew, 2006). Secondly, increased productivity results from virtual team employees spending less time commuting and in inner-office discussions (Carew & Parisi-Carew, 2006).

In light of budgetary and personnel reductions, the implementation of virtual teams may provide a means for the USAF to leverage its resources. As part of the USAF's call to transformation, the USAF must find increased levels of efficiencies by using simpler and better-integrated processes (United States Air Force, 2005). These processes require the use of new tools that streamline processes and "eliminate redundant activities" (United States Air Force, 2005, p.17). Research related to the viability of virtual teams in the USAF as a means to promote and further transformation will provide a grounded basis for the adoption of this new teaming approach.

Research Questions

This study examined the experiences of 20 virtual team members chartered by the Secretary of the USAF to facilitate organizational transformation. Members of the team were located across the continental United States, Hawaii, and Europe. To ascertain the feasibility of implementing virtual teams as a means to globalize resources and transform the organization, three research questions guided this study.

1. What positive elements of virtual team operation exist that allow them to leverage and globalize resources across the USAF, and what are the negative elements of virtual team operation that serve as potential barriers to this goal?

2. How can virtual team leadership provide a more effective means to leverage and globalize resources?

3. What should be the vision for virtual collaborative efforts that will globalize resources and secure a defense strategy?

Methodology

Data collection for this study commenced once the qualification of participants was completed. Research participants were individuals and organizations identified as team members by the AFSO21 virtual team leadership. Unstructured interviews for the collection of data sought to provide an understanding of the lived experiences (Seidman, 2006) of the AFSO21 virtual team members. The interview process provided an avenue to comprehend the meaning of behaviors by team members, and the meaning they ascribed to their actions on the team (Seidman, 2006). The capturing of these behaviors and meanings helped create the foundation to develop a virtual team implementation checklist. (Appendix A)

Data analysis used a seven-step process as developed by Moustakas (1994). This process included steps to group the data, reduce and eliminate irrelevant data, clustering, final theme identification, use of relevant themes from each participant, and construction of descriptions for the meaning of a research participant's experiences. Recordings of each interview proved the data for analysis. The creation of separate recording transcripts maintained data integrity. After the initial grouping of themes, qualitative analysis software aided in the reduction and elimination of data.

Major Findings

Analysis of the data found 13 themes related to the operation, leadership, and collaboration of virtual teams. These themes if addressed by organizations prior to the implementation of virtual teams can result in higher efficiency teams through improved collaboration, interaction, problem solving, and leadership. Detailed information regarding all themes discovered in this study is located in Appendix C.

Virtual Team Operation
Virtual teams, just like traditional face-to-face teams, need to establish a team charter and have a clear purpose. Of the 20 participants in the study 95% commented on the need for a team charter

or the lack of one as related to the AFSO21 virtual team. Additionally 70% of the participants remarked they felt the team lacked a clear purpose.

The AFSO21 team's lack of a charter left them susceptible to unclear assignments, goals, and a conflict resolution strategy.
Participant 17 commented how he or she felt the AFSO21 virtual team lacked focus on occasion, moving from topic to topic with no singular focus in efforts. Virtual teams must define the scope of their activities via a team charter. Defining the scope of the team's project ensures team members fully understand the expectations of team leadership and the sponsoring organization as they relate to the outcome of the team's efforts. The consensus a team charter provides would have reduced wasted effort and ambiguity in team member's roles.

Virtual team leaders and members need to be prepared for the challenge of operating without non-verbal communication cues.
Half of the AFSO21 virtual team members commented about the challenge of operating virtually due to the loss of nonverbal communication cues. Participant 19 remarked how team members felt they were talking to the team but were unsure they were getting their point across to their teammates. Participant 13 felt the main limitation of virtual team communication was members could not see the body language of someone speaking, and members had to rely on the volume and tone of the speaker. Additionally, this limitation sometimes resulted in placing greater emphasis on the volume and tone of the speaker over the content of what they said.

Virtual team leaders need to develop the ability to interpret the hidden cues in team member communication. In effect, virtual team leaders must be able to hear the body language of their team members despite the lack of face-to-face interaction. Doing so will allow the leader to better engage team members, ensure their concerns are received in a positive and constructive manner, and receive the appropriate attention.

Virtual teams can enhance knowledge and information sharing and leverage expertise globally.
According to one participant, the virtual team process provided him or her access to "creative solutions that other people have come up with or issues you may not have thought of." Virtual teams have the potential to increase the formation of creative solutions through the diverse talents and skills comprising the team membership.

A key part of the cross-flow of information is having the right members on the virtual team to accomplish the team's purpose. Participant 1 commented almost every Major Command in the Air Force and the leads for different organizational processes evaluated through AFSO were part of the AFSO21 virtual team. This membership allowed the AFSO21 virtual team to share ideas across the USAF, to leverage and globalize resources and produce efficiencies in organizational processes.

Virtual Team Leadership

Virtual teams require strong leadership just like their conventional face-to-face team counterparts. One unique difference for virtual teams however is team leadership may change. Seeking an understanding of how virtual team leadership can facilitate a more effective means to leverage and globalize resources was the purpose of the second research question.

Virtual team leaders need to choose an appropriate leadership style when leading virtually. The leadership style employed by the AFSO21 virtual team leader influenced the level of collaboration and the flow of information experienced in the team. Virtual team leaders need to move between various leadership approaches to ensure their team is operating at peak performance. As witnessed in this team, leadership increased effectiveness when they divided tasks through a distributive leadership style.

The application of a downward driven leadership style hinders the effectiveness of virtual teams. This leadership style proves to be an ineffective technique as mentioned by the AFSO21 virtual team members. This finding is consistent with the foundational work on virtual teams by Hambley, O'Neill, and Kline (2007).

Virtual teams need a clearly defined leader.
One unique element of virtual team leadership is the leadership of the team may change hands many times. As witnessed by the AFSO21 virtual team, the leadership of the team transitioned throughout its life cycle. While the leadership may shift during the course of the team's life cycle, a requirement still exists for the team to have a clearly defined leader. Seventy percent of the interviewed team members remarked they were not sure who the virtual team leader was.

The need for a clearly defined team leader was never accomplished by the AFSO21 virtual team and thereby undermined their potential. Team leaders need to fill a vital social role bringing together individuals from across the globe to form a single unit. Lacking a clearly defined leader inhibits the team members from collaborating and working towards a common purpose. Having a common team purpose adds to a member's sense of self-confidence and contribution.

> **"I don't think I could say who the leader is."** Participant 17
>
> **"Leadership of the virtual team, it's an interesting question. I am not sure who the leader is of the virtual team."** Participant 12
>
> **"You cannot tell who the distinct leader is."** Participant 2

Virtual team leaders may facilitate meetings in addition to traditional leadership roles.
The AFSO21 virtual team leaders actively served as facilitators ensuring each team member had the opportunity to provide input as they felt necessary. Additionally, off-line communication opportunities provided after the weekly team meetings to discuss unresolved issues with any team member.

Half of the AFSO21 virtual team members interviewed for this study mentioned the importance of the team leader facilitating the team's operation. The virtual team leader needs to ensure team meetings are productive by taking an active role in coordinating and facilitating team interactions. This approach allowed the team to get work done and promoted individuals to jump into the conversation if they had information to share.

Building organizational buy-in and support is a pre-determiner of virtual team success.
Failing to get organizational buy-in during change efforts is one of the top 15 reasons organizational change efforts fail according to Blanchard (2007). The AFSO21 virtual team members interviewed for this study mentioned USAF leadership had not gained organizational buy-in prior to embarking on the AFSO21 organizational change process. The AFSO process had the potential to implement significant transformational change initiatives throughout the USAF; however, USAF leadership turned the effort into a budget cut activity thereby devastating organizational buy-in and decreasing the number of implemented improvements.

> **"The lack of consistent communication from Air Force Leadership resulted in "negative strategic communication" and resulted in Air Force members suffering from "crisis fatigue and ultimately ignoring the program."**
> **Participant 2**

While the Chief of Staff of the Air Force initially served as a sponsor for AFSO21, his change in direction to move AFSO21 from a process reengineering focus to a budgetary focus undermined the AFSO21 virtual team's ability to have a sponsor facilitate their success. USAF leadership never established a consistent program for AFSO operations and never created buy-in at the major command level across the organizational structure. Inconsistent communication by USAF leadership undermined the ability of the team to overcome organizational resistance to change.

Virtual Team Collaboration
Virtual teams afford organizations the opportunity to collaborate globally, sharing intellectual resources from multiple locations to solve problems, while keeping costs low through the avoidance of travel related costs.

Virtual team leaders should look for opportunities to further collaboration.
Fifty-five percent of the interview participants mentioned how the team leaders could have improved collaboration on the team. Participants felt the team needed its own place to share, store, and collaborate on documents virtually. Additionally real time collaborative on-line tools

would have improved collaboration over the static status of archived data stored on CPI-MT. While Defense Connect On-line could have provided a powerful tool to work collaboratively on-line, technical difficulties prevented the team from leveraging the collaborative potential of this tool.

Another element of leveraging opportunities for collaboration is standardizing the processes a team will use to achieve its goals. Early on in the lifecycle of a virtual team, team members should define their processes and outline the expectations of team members. The AFSO21 virtual team may have missed this critical step according to Participant 10 who believes the globalization of knowledge is happening on a limited basis because each of the Commands is "doing it their own way."

The AFSO21 virtual team also needed to establish rules for communication so team members would know the most effective way to share information consistently across the globe. Using these techniques may have increased the level of collaboration experienced by the AFSO21 virtual team.

Virtual teams facilitate the globalization and leveraging of organizational resources. AFSO21 virtual team members shared information on projects they felt would work for their organization. Through the virtual team, they would contact other offices and obtain project data, projected savings, and the outcomes of various Lean events held in other areas of the USAF.

The ability to access expertise and cross-functional skills is one of the benefits of virtual teams. The AFSO21 virtual team would have subject matter experts and individuals with specific skills join the team temporarily to assist in problem solving. Team leaders also used the virtual team meetings to introduce new information and have subject matter experts educate team members.

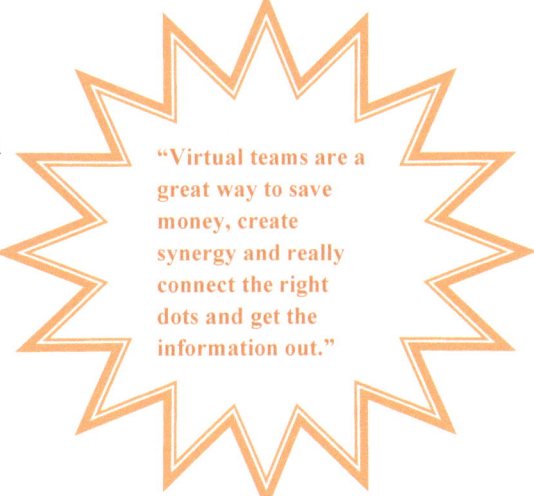

"Virtual teams are a great way to save money, create synergy and really connect the right dots and get the information out."

Sixty percent of the AFSO21 virtual team members interviewed commented on the benefit of virtual teams as a means to enhance and facilitate collaboration across the USAF. Collaborative efforts not only provided access to information across the globe but also opened doors to leverage intellectual capital in the USAF in multiple geographic locations.

"It was helpful in trying to find a creative solution that other people have come up with you may not have thought of. (Virtual teams are) a way to get to know folks within whatever area you're working across the Air Force." Participant 1

"Bang for the buck virtual teams are pretty effective. In terms of when you have geographically separated folks, you eliminate the travel time and in a lot of cases you can eliminate the time just gathering in the conference room and obviously eliminate the cost associated with travel." Participant 19

Virtual Team Sponsors

Virtual team sponsors play a vital role in determining the ultimate success or failure of a virtual team. Sponsors should consider the following areas to implement before establishing a virtual team.

Ensure the team has a clear purpose and reason for its existence.
Team sponsors should guide the development of the team charter, and hone the purpose of the team. The AFSO21 virtual team supported the Chief of Staff of the Air Force's vision for a leaner and transformed USAF. The lack of clarity on how to achieve the vision resulted in undermining the efficacy of the team in the organization however. The team's sponsorship needed to remain consistent and active throughout the AFSO21 virtual team life cycle. Doing so would have improved the team's ability to accomplish its purpose.

Establish a team leader.
The confusion AFSO21 virtual team participants had in clearly identifying the leader of the virtual team may have been a contributing factor that limited the full collaborative power of this forum. The AFSO21 virtual team demonstrated that a shared leadership approach is feasible; however, the need for a clearly defined leader still exists.

Gain organizational support.
Organizational support for change requires leadership to commit to the change efforts and take steps to achieve the desired outcomes. The lack of strategic communication resulted in organizations undermining the AFSO21 virtual team. This limited the team's influence on the overall operations of the USAF. Lacking strong support, the AFSO21 virtual team was unable to bring about true transformational change across the USAF, but had limited success in various communities and pockets of activity. With strong sponsorship, the team may have been able to influence the operations of a much wider audience.

11

Virtual Team Leaders

Team leaders whether in traditional face-to-face or virtual teams have a profound effect on how well the team will operate and accomplish the goals established at the time of its creation. Five-focus areas virtual team leaders should pay attention to presented themselves in the course of this study.

Ensure the virtual team has an agreed upon charter.
A successful team charter should clearly establish team member expectations and define the team's purpose. Some expectations a charter needs to address include how the team will address workload, resolve conflict, establish deadlines, and outline levels of commitments. The team charter should also address meeting protocols, frequency of communication, attendance requirements, team-member accountability, performance recognition, and decision-making.

Additionally, team leaders should ensure new team members read and agree to the terms of the charter before entering active membership status. The AFSO21 virtual team did not take the time to establish these elements resulting in confusion among team members relating to the expectations for attendance, communication frequency, and meeting etiquette.

Ensure the team has properly working collaborative tools.
The collaborative tools used by a virtual team are critical for effective communication for the team. On-line communication is challenging with the loss of non-verbal cues, therefore it is doubly important for team leaders to ensure the tools they are going to use for collaboration are available when needed. The AFSO21 virtual team attempted to use DCO as the primary means to share information during team meetings.

Team members reported difficulty connecting and recalled on several occasions the tool not working. Future virtual team leaders should take an active role in ensuring the tools they use have adequate technical support and will be consistently available. The use of a team sponsor who can leverage their authority to garner the requisite level of technical support needed by the team is one approach to secure a robust and viable collaborative environment for future virtual teams.

Choose an appropriate leadership style.
Virtual team leaders should seek to employ collaborative and participative leadership styles. Empowering employees through collaborative or participative leadership will result in improved employee satisfaction, performance, motivation, and stimulate followers intellectually to develop and contribute new ideas to help solve team issues. Directive leadership on the other hand, may

result in less cross-flow of information among team members as witnessed by the AFSO21 virtual team.

On occasion, the AFSO21 virtual team leadership used the directive leadership style to push information regarding ongoing issues. This resulted in shutting down communication by team members. The leaders of future USAF and DOD virtual teams should cautiously apply directive leadership only as necessary, understanding the implications it will have on team collaboration, performance, and team member's levels of motivation.

Virtual team leaders should seek to employ a collaborative leadership style to improve buy-in and motivation of virtual team members. This leadership style employs an approach that creates an atmosphere where team members feel encouraged to participate and share ideas. These ideas provide buy-in for team members increasing their level of commitment to the team.

Seek opportunities to further collaboration.
Future virtual team leaders in the USAF and DOD should consider the value in finding opportunities to further collaboration in the team environment. The AFSO21 virtual team could have improved its collaboration by using effective collaborative tools. The AFSO21 virtual team may have missed fully leveraging and globalizing resources because of system constraints imposed by CPI-MT. The limited sharing of transformational improvements across the USAF represents a missed opportunity to leverage and globalize resources.

Virtual Team Members

Virtual team members play a crucial role in helping the team succeed. Their input in selecting the best collaborative tools for the team's purpose, incorporating new team members based on their areas of expertise and helping define team member expectations are three areas uncovered that influence a team's performance.

Establish the expectations of team members early in the team's life cycle.
Virtual team members as part of the charter development process need to ensure they clearly define expectations of team members regarding several performance areas. Defining how the team will resolve conflict, the appropriate response time to questions from team mates, the accepted levels of participation, and meeting attendance are key areas virtual team members need to clarify before embarking on their chartered purpose.

Choose collaborative tools that fit the team's purpose.

Effective virtual teams employ tools that fit their needs and receive training on them. The AFSO21 virtual team suffered from the employment of communication tools that either did not function as needed or did not facilitate collaboration in a simple manner. Virtual teams should leverage information and expertise on a global level. Future virtual teams should avoid the use of tools that hamper collaboration and replace them with those that enhance team communication.

Integrate subject matter experts to leverage expertise.

The use of subject matter experts represents a high point in the collaboration of the AFSO21 virtual team. The team used subject matter experts to provide knowledge on Lean Six Sigma, and corporate business practices. As organizational leaders seek to save resources and downsize, virtual teams represent a viable teaming option that can bring together experts from across the globe into a single forum designed to leverage and globalize resources.

AFP Press. (2009). Obama seeks 663.7 bln for 2010 defense spending. Retrieved March 10,
2009, from http://www.google.com/hostednews/afp/article/
ALeqM5gjEa9Pk0c41alypgd5pBRLQ8a9RA

Blanchard, K. (2007). 15 Predictable reasons why change efforts typically fail. Retrieved January
9, 2007, from
http://www.kenblanchard.com/thoughtleadership/authors/15_reasons/Defalut.asp

Carew, D., & Parisi-Carew, E. (2006). Achieving excellence virtually: organizing, leading and
energizing high performing virtual teams. Retrieved January 10, 2007, from
http://www.kenblanchard.com/Business_Leadership/
Effective_Leadership_White_Papers/Achieving_Excellence_Virtual_Teams/Default.asp

Faykes, F. (2007). FY07 Air Force Budget. Retrieved August 4, 2007, from
http://www.globalsecurity.org/military/library/budget/fy2007/usaf/fy2007-budget-
rollout.pdf

Frost, W. (2008). Transformation in today's Air Force. *Misawa Air Base*. Retrieved February 2,
2009, from http://www.misawa.af.mil/news/story.asp?id=123117857

Garmone J., (2001). Bush calls for military transformation. *DefenseLink News*. Retrieved August
6, 2008, from http://www.defenselink.mil/Utility/
printitem.aspx?print=http:// www.defenselink.mil/news/Dec2001/

Hambley, L., O'Neill, T., & Kline, T. (2007). Virtual team leadership: perspectives from the field. *International Journal of e-Collaboration, 3*(1), 65-83. Retrieved January 4, 2008, from ProQuest database.

Haselkorn, M. (2007). Strategic management of information and communication technology: The United States Air Force Experience with Y2K. Washington, D.C.: The National Academies Press.

LaRue, B., Childs, P., & Larson, K. (2006). Leading organizations from the inside out (2nd ed.). New York, NY: John Wiley & Sons.

Miles, D. (2009). Defense leaders laud Bush at farewell ceremony. *American Forces Press Service*. Retrieved February 2, 2009, from http://www.defenselink.mil/

Moustakas, C. (1994). Phenomenological research methods. Thousand Oaks, CA: SAGE Publications.

Office of the Assistant Secretary for Public Affairs. (2005). Facing the future: meeting the threats and challenges of the 21st century. Washington, D.C.: U.S. Department of Defense.

Rubin, M. (2007). Asymmetrical threat concept and its reflections on international security. Middle East Forum. Retrieved March 10, 2009, from http://www.meforum.org/1696/asymmetrical-threat-concept-and-its-reflections

Seidman, I. (2006). Interviewing as qualitative research (3rd ed.). New York, NY: Teachers College Press.

Seymour, G., & Cowen, M. (2006). A review of team collaboration tools used in the military and

government. SPAWAR. Retrieved February 13, 2009, from

http://www.au.af.mil/au/awc/awcgate/navy/onr_review_team_collaboration.doc

United States Air Force. (2005). Air Force transformation. Retrieved August 14, 2008, from

http://www.au.af.mil/au/awc/awcgate/af/edge2005.pdf

White House. (2009). The agenda: homeland security. Retrieved January 30, 2009, from

http://www.whitehouse.gov/agenda/homeland_security/

Appendix A – Virtual Team Implementation Checklist

QUESTION	YES	NO
1. Has the team created a clearly defined and agreed upon team charter and purpose?		
2. Does the team have a strong sponsor to secure organizational buy-in and resources?		
3. Does the team have a clearly designated leader?		
4. Has the team leader been trained on virtual collaboration and leadership?		
5. Does the team have a trained and designated meeting facilitator?		
6. Has a consistent meeting schedule been established?		
7. Have team member expectations been defined? Expectations should include individual responsibilities, frequency of communication, meeting attendance, the sharing of information, and conflict resolution.		
8. Have team members been trained on behaviors that enhance or stifle collaboration?		
9. Are team members trained to deal with unique virtual team challenges? These challenges include understanding how to communicate through cultural barriers, across time zones, and the etiquette for virtual team dialogue.		
10. Is the team prepared to communicate without non-verbal cues?		
11. Is there a plan to ensure new members are incorporated during the team's life cycle?		
12. Did the team select the collaborative tools that best fit their purpose?		
13. Has training been provided on the collaborate tools to the team members?		
14. Have the team's collaborative tools been tested prior to implementation?		
15. Is there a plan to keep up with new technology that can influence collaboration?		

A review of the study's demographics provides insight into how well the sample population represented the AFSO21 virtual team's overall membership. The AFSO21 team roster (SAF/SO, 2007a) listed 41 members currently participating in team activities. Of these members, 36 were Air Force Officers, 27 were civilian employees, 2 contractors, and 5 team members were enlisted members in the Air Force (see Figure 1).

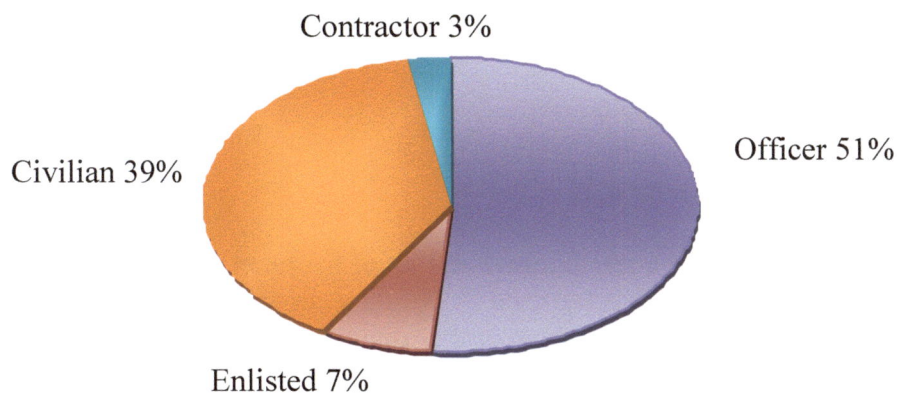

Figure 1. AFSO21 virtual team demographics.

Additionally, the team membership included representatives from every Major Command in the USAF. The researcher extended an invitation to participate in the study to at least one virtual team member from each major command. For those commands with more than one team member, a random number generator assigned a value to each team member. The team member invited first had the highest random number. If the member declined, an invitation was extended to another individual within the same organization with the next highest random number to participate in the research effort.

In the case of two major commands, no team members agreed to participate in the research effort. In these instances, another organization on the virtual team was selected using the same random number generation technique described above. During the invitation process, demographics were not a factor of consideration in sample population selection. The random number generation process was the only factor applied to select the potential sample population to avoid any potential biases in choosing interview subjects. Despite the random approach used to invite team members, the demographics of the sample population closely mirror those of the team. The sample size of N = 20 was comprised of 10 officers, 9 civilian employees, and 1 contractor (see Figure 2).

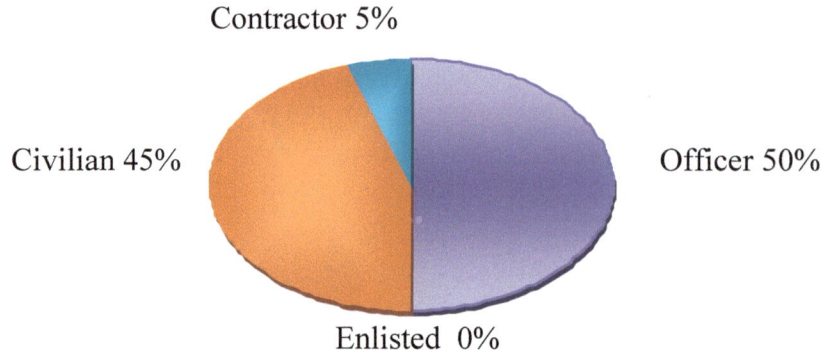

Figure 2. Sample population demographics.

The only deviation from the sample population and that of the team membership was with enlisted members. Enlisted members comprised 7% of the team; however, they were not represented in the sample population. Evaluating the invitations extended to team members revealed two enlisted team members were invited to participate in the study, however both declined.

Table 1

Positive elements of virtual team operation

	Time & Travel Savings	% of Sample	Cross-flow of Information	% of Sample	Dollar Savings	% of Sample	Leverage Expertise	% of Sample
Positive Elements (N = 20)	2	10%	14	70%	9	45%	5	25%

Note. Data represents the number of respondents who specifically mentioned each theme as it related to the positive elements of virtual team operation. Therefore, the total number of responses in the table may be less than, equal to, or more than the sample population.

Table 2

Negative elements of virtual team operation

	Tool & Connectivity Issues	% of Sample	Loss of Nonverbal Communication	% of Sample	Collaboration Challenges	% of Sample
Negative Elements (N = 20)	7	35%	10	50%	5	25%

Note. Data represents the number of respondents who specifically mentioned each theme as it related to the negative elements of virtual team operation. Therefore, the total number of responses in the table may be less than, equal to, or more than the sample population.

Table 3

Influence of military culture on virtual team performance

	Positive Influence	% of Sample	Negative Influence	% of Sample	Neutral Influence	% of Sample
Military Culture (N = 20)	0	0%	3	15%	14	70%

Note. Data represents the number of respondents who specifically mentioned each theme as it related to the influence of military culture on virtual team performance. Therefore, the total number of responses in the table may be less than, equal to, or more than the sample population.

Table 4

Influence of Air Force culture on virtual team performance

	Positive Influence	% of Sample	Negative Influence	% of Sample	Neutral Influence	% of Sample
Military Culture (N = 20)	4	20%	8	40%	0	0%

Note. Data represents the number of respondents who specifically mentioned each theme as it related to the influence of Air Force culture on virtual team performance. Therefore, the total number of responses in the table may be less than, equal to, or more than the sample population.

Table 5

Influence of face-to-face meetings on virtual team operation

	Positive Influence	% of Sample	Negative Influence	% of Sample	Neutral Influence	% of Sample
Face-to face Meetings (N = 20)	5	25%	3	15%	0	0%

Note. Data represents the number of respondents who specifically mentioned each theme as it related to the influence of face-to-face meetings on virtual team operation. Therefore, the total number of responses in the table may be less than, equal to, or more than the sample population.

Table 6

Team expectations influencing performance

	Attendance	% of Sample	Conduct During Meetings	% of Sample
Expectations Defined (N = 20)	7	35%	3	15%

Note. Data represents the number of respondents who specifically mentioned each theme as it related to the expectations influencing virtual team performance. Therefore, the total number of responses in the table may be less than, equal to, or more than the sample population.

Table 7

Role of clear team purpose as influencer on virtual team performance

	Team Charter	% of Sample	Unclear Purpose	% of Sample
Clear Purpose (N = 20)	19	95%	14	70%

Note. Data represents the number of respondents who specifically mentioned each theme as it related to the role of a clear team purpose as an influence on virtual team performance. Therefore, the total number of responses in the table may be less than, equal to, or more than the sample population.

Table 8

Tools as influencing factors of virtual team operation

	Tools not Working	% of Sample	Hard to Use	% of Sample	Barriers to Collaboration	% of Sample	Adequate Tools	% of Sample
Collaboration Tools (N = 20)	7	35%	8	40%	6	30%	8	40%

Note. Data represents the number of respondents who specifically mentioned each theme as it related to tools as influencing factors on virtual team performance. Therefore, the total number of responses in the table may be less than, equal to, or more than the sample population.

Table 9

Leadership as positive influence on virtual team performance

	Leader as Facilitator	% of Sample	Choosing Correct Leadership Style	% of Sample
Leadership (N = 20)	10	50%	19	95%

Note. Data represents the number of respondents who specifically mentioned each theme as it related to the positive influence of leadership on virtual team performance. Therefore, the total number of responses in the table may be less than, equal to, or more than the sample population.

Table 10

Leadership as negative influence on virtual team performance

	Lacking Vision	% of Sample	Not Seeking Buy-in	% of Sample	No Defined Leader	% of Sample
Leadership (N = 20)	10	50%	10	50%	14	70%

Note. Data represents the number of respondents who specifically mentioned each theme as it related to the negative influence of leadership on virtual team performance. Therefore, the total number of responses in the table may be less than, equal to, or more than the sample population.

Table 11

Positive elements of virtual team collaboration

	Strong Collaboration	% of Sample	Opportunities to Enhance Collaboration	% of Sample
Collaboration (N = 20)	12	60%	11	55%

Note. Data represents the number of respondents who specifically mentioned each theme as it related to the positive elements of virtual team collaboration. Therefore, the total number of responses in the table may be less than, equal to, or more than the sample population.

Table 12

Negative elements of virtual team collaboration.

	Team Meeting Format	% of Sample	Limited Collaboration	% of Sample
Collaboration (N = 20)	13	65%	5	25%

Note. Data represents the number of respondents who specifically mentioned each theme as it related to the negative elements of virtual team collaboration. Therefore, the total number of responses in the table may be less than, equal to, or more than the sample population.